DISCARD

ROBERTO CLEMENTE

By David Fischer

WORLD ALMANAC® LIBRARY

Please visit our web site at: www.worldalmanaclibrary.com
For a free color catalog describing World Almanac® Library's list
of high-quality books and multimedia programs, call 1-800-848-2928 (USA)
or 1-800-387-3178 (Canada). World Almanac® Library's fax: (414) 332-3567.

Library of Congress Cataloging-in-Publication Data

Fischer, David, 1963-
    Roberto Clemente / by David Fischer.
      p. cm. — (Trailblazers of the modern world)
    Includes bibliographical references and index.
    ISBN 0-8368-5495-0 (lib. bdg.)
    ISBN 0-8368-5264-8 (softcover)
    1. Clemente, Roberto, 1934-1972—Juvenile literature. 2. Baseball players—Puerto Rico—
Biography—Juvenile literature. I. Title. II. Series.
GV865.C439F57   2004
796.357'092—dc22
[B]   2004041289

First published in 2005 by
World Almanac® Library
330 West Olive Street, Suite 100
Milwaukee, WI 53212 USA

Copyright © 2005 by World Almanac® Library.

Project manager: Jonny Brown
Editor: Alan Wachtel
Design and page production: Scott M. Krall
Photo research: Diane Laska-Swanke
Indexer: Walter Kronenberg

Photo credits: © AP/Wide World Photos: 8 bottom, 21, 28, 30; © Bettmann/CORBIS: cover, 4, 5, 10, 11, 13, 17, 19, 22, 23, 24, 25, 26, 27, 31, 32, 33, 34, 36, 38, 39, 40, 41, 42, 43; Scott M. Krall/© World Almanac Library, 2005: 6; © Thomas D. Mcavoy/Time Life Pictures/Getty Images: 7; © George Silk/Time Life Pictures/Getty Images: 14, 18, 29, 37; © Underwood & Underwood/CORBIS: 8 top

All rights reserved. No part of this book may be reproduced, stored in a retrieval system, or transmitted in any form or by any means, electronic, mechanical, photocopying, recording, or otherwise, without the prior written permission of the copyright holder.

Printed in the United States of America.

1 2 3 4 5 6 7 8 9 08 07 06 05 04

TABLE of CONTENTS

CHAPTER 1	A GENUINE SUPERSTAR		4
CHAPTER 2	A BALL FIELD IN THE BARRIO		7
CHAPTER 3	THE ROAD TO PITTSBURGH		13
CHAPTER 4	EARLY YEARS WITH THE PIRATES		20
CHAPTER 5	COMING OF AGE		26
CHAPTER 6	LEADING BY EXAMPLE		32
CHAPTER 7	HITTING THE BIG TIME		39
	TIMELINE		44
	GLOSSARY		45
	TO FIND OUT MORE		46
	INDEX		47

Words that appear in the glossary are printed in **boldface** type the first time they occur in the text.

CHAPTER 1

A GENUINE SUPERSTAR

Roberto Clemente after smashing one of his 3,000 career hits

On September 30, 1972, Roberto Clemente of the Pittsburgh Pirates stepped into the batter's box at Pittsburgh's Three Rivers Stadium and made **major league baseball** history. Facing the New York Mets' pitcher John Matlack, Clemente smashed a hard line drive off the wall for a double. It was the 3,000th hit of Clemente's baseball career—a mark reached only by the best hitters in the game. In more than one hundred years of major league baseball, only twenty-four players have had 3,000 or more hits.

A TRULY GREAT PLAYER

During his eighteen-year major league career, Clemente hit .300 or better in thirteen seasons, won four batting titles, and won twelve Gold Glove awards. He led his team to victory the only two times it reached the World Series, and he hit well in the clutch, or when it matters most. Clemente was a complete ball player. He could run, throw, field, and hit with the best. The legendary sportswriter Roger Angell said that Clemente played "something close to the level of absolute perfection."

PRIDE OF PUERTO RICO

Born in Puerto Rico and always maintaining ties to the island, Roberto Clemente is the most popular sports figure in the island's history. His charitable acts are legendary around the world, and his face has appeared on postage stamps and his name on a sports complex for poor children in Puerto Rico. Always willing to extend a hand to help people in need, Clemente mentored other young Hispanic ballplayers in Pittsburgh, helping them adjust to life in a foreign country. Clemente's leadership and his caring were shining examples to everyone. During his career, he earned the respect of his teammates as a passionate leader and the admiration of many fans for his compassionate nature. His impact off the field was as big as his play on the diamond.

This Roberto Clemente commemorative stamp was issued by the United States Postal Service in 1984.

Today, Clemente is remembered for being one of the few true heroes American baseball has ever produced, as well as for being one of baseball's most exciting players. While his baseball success brought great pride to all Spanish-speaking people, Clemente traveled a very lonely road during the early years of his career. He was often the only Spanish-speaking player on his team and, particularly early in his career, always one of the few blacks in all of the major leagues. When opponents taunted him, he could not always understand the insults, but he knew the words were purposefully hurtful. Yet despite being an outsider, Clemente achieved extraordinary success in a pressure-packed profession under difficult circumstances.

ON AND OFF THE FIELD

After establishing himself as a star player, Clemente believed that it was his duty to work for social equality in all areas of American life. At times, his words sparked controversy, and critics resented his complaints on topics ranging from injuries to injustice. Through it all, he was honest and determined that his voice be heard.

In today's world, where athletes regularly shrug off their responsibilities to be role models, Clemente's commitment and dedication to helping others is unmatched. An inspiration to baseball fans and nonbaseball fans, Clemente once said: "Anytime you have an opportunity to make things better and you don't, then you are wasting your time on this Earth."

The Shining Star

Puerto Rico is the smallest of the Greater Antilles Islands, which include Cuba (the largest), the Dominican Republic, Haiti, and Jamaica. Located about 1,000 miles (1,600 kilometers) south of Miami, Florida, it is surrounded by the Atlantic Ocean to the north and the Caribbean Sea to the south. Puerto Rico was explored by Christopher Columbus on his second voyage to the New World in 1493 and claimed for Spain. A territory of the United States since 1898, the island became the Commonwealth of Puerto Rico in 1952. As a commonwealth, Puerto Rico governs itself but keeps close ties to the United States.

A BALLFIELD IN THE BARRIO

CHAPTER 2

Roberto Clemente Walker—his full name, keeping with the Hispanic custom of placing the mother's maiden name last—was born in the small **barrio** of San Anton in Carolina, Puerto Rico, on August 18, 1934. The village was like many of the small farming towns in the rural United States in that it had many poor people who worked very hard in the fields and also many people without jobs. The Clemente family was better off than many of their neighbors.

A typical family of Puerto Rican sugar plantation workers sitting outside their shack

SUGAR CANE AND OXCARTS

Roberto's parents, Luisa and Melchor Clemente, worked long hours on a sugarcane plantation called the Victoria Sugar Mill. Melchor was a foreman in the factory and Luisa worked in the laundry, cleaning the workers' clothes. Their jobs did not make them rich—they earned less than one dollar a day—but gave them enough money to support their eight children. Roberto was the youngest child. He had five older brothers and two older sisters. He depended on them when his parents were away from the house, and he relied on them when he needed a friend. As the baby in a large family, Roberto

Workers transporting harvested sugarcane from the fields to a factory using oxcarts.

always had someone to play with. One of his fondest early memories was bouncing along the dirt roads of Carolina, riding in an oxcart pushed by one of his siblings.

The Clemente family lived inside a modest one-story, wooden house with a tin roof. The space may have been cramped, but there was room for everyone. Surviving mainly on a diet of rice and beans, the family spent their evenings gathered around the dinner table talking about the day's events, sharing jokes and laughing together. When food got scarce, Melchor and Luisa let their children eat first and then they would eat whatever, if anything, was left over. The young Roberto was keenly aware that his parents were making enormous sacrifices for him and his older siblings. This made him feel secure and safe, and it taught him the importance of family.

STRONG FAMILY ROOTS

Melchor and Luisa Clemente (left) taught Roberto the importance of family.

At the time of Roberto's birth, Melchor was fifty-four years old. During the time when Melchor worked as a manager of a grocery store, Roberto helped his father load and unload trucks. It was during these times that Melchor would talk to his youngest son about honor and dignity. He taught Roberto always to be proud of his Puerto Rican heritage and advised him never to forget who he was and where he came from. Roberto respected and admired his father, and these lessons inspired him and shaped his character.

Luisa Clemente drew great strength from her spiritual beliefs and attended church regularly. She often took Roberto with her to the Baptist services in Carolina. While most Puerto Ricans follow the teachings of Roman Catholicism—and Roberto would eventually marry in the Catholic church—his mother's Baptist faith helped to instill in him a strong set of morals and values.

"I owe so much to my parents," Roberto said. "They did so much for me. I never heard my father or mother raise their voices in our home. I never heard hate in my house."

FINDING HIMSELF

Roberto Clemente loved baseball more than anything. Beginning at the age of five, he began hitting tin cans with a stick and throwing rocks at nearby trees. Whenever his mother sent him on errands, he would return home hours later, all dirty from playing ball.

"Baseball was my whole life," Roberto said. "We played all day and I wouldn't care if we missed lunch. We played until it was too dark to see."

The Clemente family never had money to spend on luxury items like toys, but that didn't stop the children from playing games. Like so many poor young kids in Latin American countries, Roberto made a baseball glove out of cardboard milk cartons, a bat out of a tree branch, and a ball out of a rolled-up sock with tape tightly wrapped around it.

The early years of Clemente's life were times of self-reliance. When he was nine years old he wanted a bicycle. His father told him he would have to earn it. Roberto

Jackie Robinson, the first black major league ballplayer, gave hope to all minority athletes.

El Béisbol

Baseball is an important part of the culture of Puerto Rico, where the endless summer allows baseball games to be played all year round. The game came to the island in 1900, introduced by United States soldiers who were stationed there after the Spanish-American War. Although it's often called "America's national pastime," in Latin American countries such as Puerto Rico, where there are hundreds of local teams to follow, *el béisbol* is even more popular and the fans even more enthusiastic than in the United States.

The Puerto Rican League has attracted many of the best Latino baseball players to the island since 1938. For many of these young men, professional baseball is a way out of poverty. Yet some of the best Spanish-speaking players never gained the worldwide fame they deserved. When Roberto Clemente was a boy, major league baseball in the United States was restricted to white men only. At the time, black players participated in the Negro Leagues during the summer, and during the winter played in the Puerto Rican League. Not until Clemente was thirteen years old could a dark-skinned athlete dream of coming to the United States to play before sold-out crowds in Boston's Fenway Park or New York's Yankee Stadium. What made the dream possible was that on April 15, 1947, a black American named Jackie Robinson made history by playing in the major leagues as a member of the Brooklyn Dodgers.

found a neighbor who needed someone to carry heavy, metal milk cans to a store half a mile away, fill them with milk, and bring them back. Every morning before school, Roberto filled and carried the milk cans. He was paid a few pennies each time, and after three long years, he had finally earned the money he needed to buy a used bike.

THE YOUNG ATHLETE

Luisa and Melchor Clemente always told their children that a good education was the way to a better life in Puerto Rico. They hoped their youngest child would one day be an engineer. Roberto always acted with respect toward his teachers and behaved well in class, but school

A Special Friendship

Roberto rode his second-hand bicycle to Sixto Escobar Stadium in the capital city of San Juan, Puerto Rico, where he would watch his favorite players through the outfield fence. The one that most impressed him was Monte Irvin, a Negro League outfielder who played for the San Juan Senators during the Puerto Rican Winter League season.

"I used to wait in front of the ballpark just for him to pass by, so I could see him," recalled Clemente.

After several visits to the ballpark, and countless autograph requests, Roberto and Irvin formed a special friendship. Roberto would carry Irvin's glove for him, and in return, Irvin would give Roberto used baseballs and broken bats. Clemente and Irvin remained close friends throughout their lives.

Monte Irvin was Roberto Clemente's favorite player when Roberto was a boy.

did not come easy for him. His mind was always on baseball. And when he wasn't playing, he would bounce a rubber ball and squeeze it to strengthen his arm.

By the time he was a young teenager, the villagers of Carolina were abuzz with talk of Clemente's impressive baseball skills. Word reached a man named Roberto Marín, who then spotted Clemente whacking tin cans with a wooden bat made from a guava tree limb. Marín was in charge of a softball team sponsored by the Sello Rojo [SELL-oh ROH-ho] Rice Company. Noticing that Clemente's glove was made from an old coffee sack, Marín recruited Roberto for the team by offering him an old leather glove. After getting permission from his parents, Roberto joined the team. Despite playing with and competing against men nearly twice his age, the 14-year-old **phenomenon** was the shining star on the diamond. He played shortstop but was soon moved to right field to take advantage of his strong throwing arm.

A Medal-Winning Javelin Thrower

While baseball was his favorite sport, Roberto also excelled at track and field while at Vizcarrondo High School. He was a medal-winning **javelin** thrower and was briefly considered to be among the athletes who could represent Puerto Rico in the 1952 summer Olympics in Helsinki, Finland. Roberto, however, decided to concentrate on baseball, but javelin throwing helped him further develop his throwing arm.

THE ROAD TO PITTSBURGH

CHAPTER 3

In 1952, Clemente earned a tryout with a professional team in the Puerto Rican League called the Santurce Cangrejeros [kahn-gray-HARE-ose], or Crabbers. At the tryout, he played like a man possessed, making diving catches on his belly and sliding into the bases like an avalanche. The owner of the team immediately signed Roberto to a contract that paid him a salary of $40 a month.

As the 1952-1953 season began, Roberto did not get much playing time. Instead, he sat on the bench and watched. With so many veteran players in the winter leagues, his manager did not want Clemente to become

Roberto Clemente wearing his first professional uniform as a member of the Santurce Crabbers in 1952

Learning from the Pros

James Buster "Buzz" Clarkson had been a star in the Negro Leagues and had become a legendary player in the Puerto Rican Winter League. By the winter of 1952, he was also managing the Santurce Crabbers. Clarkson encouraged his young outfielder, telling Clemente that he would eventually become a star in the United States.

"He had a few rough spots," Clarkson said, "but he never made the same mistake twice. He was baseball savvy and he listened."

13

discouraged playing against older, more experienced players. So Roberto watched and learned—and practiced. He was determined to improve his skills.

SHOWING PROMISE

Roberto worked tirelessly in batting practice to learn to hit the pitches that gave him difficulty. By 1953, he was playing regularly in the Santurce outfield and attracting the attention of several U.S. teams because of his hitting, fielding, and throwing abilities.

The winter was a time when many of the big stars from the United States major leagues and the Negro Leagues played in Puerto Rico with the best players from that country. In the winter of 1953, the Santurce Crabbers fielded an outfield of nineteen-year-old Roberto Clemente, Willie Mays, the young New York Giants star three seasons into his majestic career, and veteran Negro League star Bob Thurman. Some winter-league fans called Santurce's 1953 outfield the best they had ever seen. Clemente batted .355 that season, and the trio of Clemente, Mays, and Thurman led Santurce to victory in the Puerto Rican Winter League championship.

Soon after the victory, the Brooklyn Dodgers **scout** Al Campanis held a clinic, and Clemente wowed him with his impressive skills. Campanis convinced the Dodgers to offer Clemente a $10,000 bonus to play for them. That was more money than Roberto's parents could earn in twenty years. The teenager had to wait until he graduated from high school before he could sign

Willie Mays teamed with Clemente to lead the Santurce Crabbers to the Puerto Rican Winter League title in 1953.

14

with a major league team, but he gave his word to Campanis that he would sign with the Dodgers. There were other teams, notably the Milwaukee Braves, who came in with offers at least three times higher. Facing an important decision and not sure what he should do, Roberto sought his parents' advice. They told their son that a person's promise is a sacred trust, and since he had already given his word to the Brooklyn club, he must not back out.

Roberto signed a contract with the Dodgers and was told to report to the team's spring training camp in Vero Beach, Florida, in February 1954. Leaving home for the first time, he was determined to make his country proud. He wanted to show that other young athletes from the Caribbean Islands could make it to the major leagues.

EARLY YEAR STRUGGLES

Instead of following the Dodgers to Brooklyn's Ebbets Field to start the 1954 regular season as he had expected, Roberto Clemente was shipped to the minor leagues. He was assigned to play for the Montreal Royals in the International League.

Life in Canada required a major adjustment for Clemente. Unlike the sizzling hot temperatures of his native Puerto Rico, the weather in Canada is cold and snowy for much of the year. Luckily, the people of Montreal were warm and welcoming. Fans of the Royals cheered Clemente's electrifying play, but the Hispanic teenager didn't get very many opportunities to showcase his abilities.

By sending Clemente down to their **farm team**, the Dodgers were actually taking a big risk, and they knew it. A rule required that if a team paid a large bonus to a player, he must remain on the major league roster. If not, any team could claim that player for themselves in a postseason draft. Since the Dodgers already had great outfielders at the major league level, they were "hiding" their young star from other teams.

In one of his first games at Delorimier Downs, Montreal's home ballpark, Clemente rocketed a home run that sailed clear out of the stadium. No other Royals player had ever hit such a titanic homer. And yet the next day he was sitting on the bench. This odd treatment from his manager, Max Macon, confused Clemente, and the situation was never fully explained to him.

"I Was Mad"

Reflecting on his only season of minor league ball, Clemente said, "If I struck out I stay in the lineup," he said. "If I played well I'm benched. One day I hit three triples and the next day I was benched. Another time they took me out for a pinch hitter with the bases loaded in the first inning. Much of the time I was used only as a pinch runner or for defense. I didn't know what was going on. I was mad."

The lack of playing time annoyed him. But sitting on the bench was not as humiliating to Clemente as the abuse he received on his first road trip when the team traveled to Richmond, Virginia. There, Roberto encountered for the first time a problem far more personal. Unfortunately, it was not limited to the baseball field.

RACIAL INEQUALITY

Roberto Clemente discovered that the United States was not always friendly to people of color. For decades, black U.S. citizens did not enjoy the same rights and privileges as white citizens. Even though the Fourteenth Amendment, adopted in 1868, guaranteed equal treatment to blacks, many social inequalities still existed. Black Americans did not have the same job opportunities as whites, and they were often the victims of small-minded **racists**.

Whites and blacks were required to use separate water fountains in the segregated southern United States.

Racial **discrimination** was a serious social problem throughout the nation. Throughout the South, blacks and whites were kept separate in schools and in restaurants. Black Americans were forced to sit in the backs of public buses, in separate sections of stadiums, and in the balconies of movie theaters. They even had to drink from different water fountains and sleep in separate hotels. As a dark-skinned Puerto Rican man, Clemente was subjected to the same **bigotry** and second-class treatment that black U.S. citizens received. This situation offended Clemente.

Black Men on a White Team

Al Jackson, a black pitcher, was one of Clemente's first roommates. He later recalled, "We had to live in homes with black families. It was galling to Roberto, who was a big star and a hero back in Puerto Rico, when he could not stay at the hotel or eat with the white players. We had to stay on the bus while they went into a restaurant. We were not part of the team except on the field."

Branch Rickey, shown here with his grandson, had helped make baseball history in the 1940s by bringing Jackie Robinson to the Brooklyn Dodgers and breaking baseball's color barrier. Following the 1954 season, as general manager of the Pittsburgh Pirates, he beat his old team to the punch and made Roberto Clemente the first pick in the major league draft.

STRANGER IN A STRANGE LAND

Roberto Clemente barely understood English and spoke even less. He was at a tremendous disadvantage in interviews because they were conducted in an unfamiliar language. Clemente was proud of his Latino roots, and he could get very defensive about the unfair way in which he was portrayed by the media. The sportswriters had trouble understanding him, and his quotes in newspapers often contained grammatical errors that he found embarrassing and disrespectful toward all Spanish-speaking people.

Communication barriers also left him uneasy in his own locker room. Because of his limited English vocabulary, Clemente remained distant from his teammates, who mistook his silence for arrogance. Even though he worked hard to

18

improve his English, the new language was difficult for him to learn. "He was in a cultural twilight zone," said Nellie King, a sympathetic teammate.

Feeling homesick, Clemente seriously considered quitting. In the end, though, he decided to persevere in the hopes that opportunity would find him. Sure enough, despite the Dodgers' attempts to keep his profile low, Clyde Sukeforth, a scout for the Pittsburgh Pirates, had been following Clemente's career closely. He told Branch Rickey, the Pirates general manager, "You will never live long enough to draft a boy with this kind of ability again." After the 1954 season, the Pirates grabbed Clemente in the first pick of the draft. The Dodgers were helpless—they had gambled and lost.

A hustling Roberto Clemente slides into home plate during his rookie season in 1955.

CHAPTER 4
EARLY YEARS WITH THE PIRATES

The Name Game

The Pittsburgh Pirates had been called the Alleghenies until 1891. That year, they were accused of stealing a player from the Philadelphia Athletics. The Athletics had accidentally left second baseman Lou Bierbauer off a list of players who were protected from being claimed by other teams. When Pittsburgh claimed Bierbauer, the Athletics called the Alleghenies "pirates" for stealing him. The nickname stuck. The Pirates are also sometimes called the Bucs—short for *buccaneers*, another word for pirates.

When Clemente moved to Pittsburgh in 1955 to begin his **rookie** season in the big leagues, he did not even know where Pennsylvania was. It was only one year since the first Pirates' African-American player, Curt Roberts, had suited up. When Clemente arrived, he found few blacks living in or around the city and no signs at all of a Hispanic community.

Nevertheless, he was glad finally to be on a team that wanted him, and back home in Puerto Rico, his family and friends were excited. As one of the first players from Puerto Rico to join a major league team, many people there admired Clemente before he even played his first game in the Pirates' black and gold uniform. Showing a loyalty to his heritage, the number he chose to wear on the back of his jersey was "21" because there are twenty-one letters in his full name. But as big a hero as he was in Puerto Rico, fans in Pittsburgh wondered when this young star would live up to his potential. In his first season, Clemente batted just .255, with five home runs and 47 runs batted in. The young Clemente was an undisciplined hitter who rarely reached base safely, even by a walk. He walked only 18 times in 474 at bats.

"I go to the plate to hit, not to walk," he said.

The Pirates' rookie right fielder wanted immediate success and demanded perfection. But in baseball, even the best batters make outs between six and seven times out of ten. Clemente was struggling for the first time in his life, and he couldn't easily cope. He was not yet as old as the "21" on the back of his jersey, and he still had a lot of growing up to do.

GREAT GLOVE MAN

Despite an inconsistent rookie season at bat, Roberto Clemente's defensive abilities never suffered. He could track down nearly any ball hit his way, and because of his fantastic instincts, even some balls that weren't. He once fielded a bunt that had rolled to shortstop and threw out a runner at third base. Clemente's most feared weapon, however, was his rifle arm. From a distance of about 420 feet, he once threw out a runner at home plate, on one bounce.

"Clemente could field a ball in Pennsylvania and throw out a runner in New York," said longtime broadcaster Vin Scully.

Clemente honed his throwing accuracy with

Roberto Clemente robbing a hit with an acrobatic catch in right field

hours of target practice. He would take a garbage can and put it at third base with the opening facing him. A coach would hit a ball to him in right field, he would run in, scoop up the ball, and try to throw it one-hop into the garbage can.

"Tough to do," said teammate Willie Stargell. "But that's what made him shine a little brighter, stand a little taller."

Vera Clemente accepting the Gold Glove Award won by her husband in 1972

A Record-setting Fielder

Clemente had a lifetime total of 266 **assists**, the most of any modern-day outfielder. He led the league in assists five times during his career. No player in major-league history has ever led his league in assists as many times as Clemente. Runners wisely did not test his arm very often, making his assists total all the more impressive.

The Gold Glove Award is given to the most outstanding fielder at each position. Clemente won twelve Gold Gloves in a row, a record for outfielders he shares with Willie Mays.

EMOTIONAL TIMES

In his first five years in the majors, Roberto never hit more than seven home runs or knocked in more than 60 runs in a season, and his batting average rose above .300 only once. Knowing that a minority player needed more talent than a white player to be in the starting lineup, Clemente was worried that his job might be in jeopardy. Meanwhile, his team regularly finished near the bottom of the National League standings.

Clemente had a hard time accepting failure, both his own and his team's. As the losses mounted, so too did the pressures of trying to adjust to a foreign country, with its problems of racial inequality, and to fit in with new teammates who spoke a different language. As Clemente grew lonelier and his frustrations built up, he sometimes exploded with anger—throwing batting helmets to the ground, punching water coolers, and kicking dirt at umpires. Once, he even threw a punch at an umpire, for which he was ejected from the game, fined $250, and suspended for five days.

A frustrated Roberto Clemente arguing with an umpire as a teammate tries to calm him down

SERIES OF UPS AND DOWNS

During Roberto Clemente's sixth major league season, in 1960, he finally blossomed into an all-around player. He batted .314, hit 16 home runs, and led his team with 94 runs batted in. More important, he helped the Pirates win their first National League **pennant** in 33 years. The 1960 World Series against the mighty New York Yankees was one of the most dramatic ever played. After six games, each team had won three times. In the seventh and deciding game, the Pirates' second baseman Bill Mazeroski hit perhaps the most famous home run in

A joyous Bill Mazeroski greeting teammates and fans after his World Series-winning home run in 1960

baseball history. He led off the bottom of the ninth inning with a homer that won the game—and the Series—for the Pirates.

Clemente had played well in the 1960 World Series, batting .310 and getting more hits than any other Pirates player. In Game Seven, with the championship trophy on the line, he had kept a key eighth inning rally alive with a hustling infield single, that helped to set up Mazeroski's game-winning heroics. After the triumph, the Pirates celebrated wildly in the locker room. But Clemente was not there whooping it up with his teammates. He wanted to share the excitement with the fans—the working people of Pittsburgh who spend their hard-earned dollars to buy tickets to watch the Pirates play. They had waited thirty-five years for a world championship team, and Clemente knew they had been starving for a winner. He dressed quickly and stepped outside the stadium to sign autographs and shake hands.

As soon as the confetti was cleared off the streets, the Pittsburgh newspapers called into question Clemente's decision not to participate in the clubhouse celebration. Sportswriters hinted that he was purposely trying to stand apart from his teammates.

SPEAKING HIS MIND

Back home in Puerto Rico for the winter, Clemente took it hard when he got the news that he had finished a distant eighth in the balloting for the 1960 Most Valuable Player (MVP) award. As the most consistent of the Pirates' players, he thought he should have gotten more credit for their success. One of his teammates, the shortstop Dick Groat, earned the award despite missing the last month of the season with an injury. Two other Pirates also finished higher than Clemente. He was not jealous of his teammates, but he was stunned that the writers regarded him no higher than the fourth most important player on his team.

For Roberto, this snub was more evidence of what he already was beginning to believe: that Latino players could not get a fair shake from the media in the United States. Always a proud man, Clemente considered his poor showing in the MVP voting to be an insult by the writers, who select the winner. Offended by their low opinion of his value to the 1960 Pirates, Clemente swore never to wear his World Series championship ring, and he never did.

Clemente and the Press

Writers often criticized Clemente's flashy style of play, calling it showboating. On routine high fly balls, he used the low basket catch, allowing the ball to drop below his waist before snatching it. And when fielding routine singles he would sometimes underhand the ball to second base in a lazy arc instead of whipping it in a line. These were habits he had acquired while playing softball as a teenager. But the stodgy writers did not approve of these "colorful" moves and tagged Clemente a showoff.

Roberto Clemente hugging his mother, Luisa, upon returning to Puerto Rico after the 1961 season

CHAPTER 5

COMING OF AGE

The disappointment he felt over not winning the MVP award was a turning point for Clemente, who was now determined to prove the writers wrong. The next season, in 1961, he emerged as a solid and disciplined hitter. No longer swinging wildly at pitches over his head or down by his ankles, he now waited patiently for good pitches and then belted line drives, spraying them in all directions. He finished the 1961 season with a .351 average, making history as the first player from Puerto Rico to win a batting title.

Roberto Clemente's aggressive playing style often led to injury.

SORE SUBJECT

The Pirates did not repeat as world champions, and despite Clemente's best efforts over the next five seasons, the team could do no better than a third-place finish. While playing for Pittsburgh, Clemente suffered several injuries and even some serious illnesses. Frequently injured due to his aggressive style of play, he often moaned about aches and pains in his ankles, knees, legs, back, neck, and shoulders. "My bad shoulder feels good, but my good shoulder feels bad," he once said.

26

Clemente's first—and worst—injury to his back caused him to perform an oddly amusing ritual each time he entered the batters' box. Rolling his neck, head, and shoulders every which way to make sure the muscles were loose, he was always fidgety at the plate, looking like a man who was never comfortable in his own skin.

Clemente's honesty about his injuries caused him some problems. He spoke out when he was hurt during a time when many players thought playing hurt and not talking about it was honorable. Sportswriters tired of his constant bellyaching and accused Clemente of being a **hypochondriac**. Even his manager, Danny Murtaugh, would at times question his motivation for complaining. Though Clemente played in more games in a Pirates' uniform than any other player, the label of "loafer" and "faker" unjustly stuck to him. The more he complained, however, the better he played.

Roberto Clemente with Pirates manager Danny Murtaugh, who did not always understand his star player's motivation for complaining

Cultural Differences

Clemente did not like to play when his abilities were below par. His teammate Nellie King understood.

Clemente's pride would not allow him to give a bad performance. In the United States, if you don't feel good, you're supposed to go out there, put some tobacco juice on it and [say], "Let's get going." We expect that from everybody. Teammates did not understand why he was acting the way he was, or why he didn't play. It wasn't an act; it was just a sincere belief on his part. It's hard for anybody to understand that unless you understand the pride and culture he came from. He said, "If I cannot play well, I will embarrass myself and my family and I will embarrass the team."

MEETING VERA

In the days before satellite television, the people of Puerto Rico had little chance to watch their baseball heroes perform in the United States. So once the baseball season ended Clemente always returned home to play the winter season in the Puerto Rican League.

In the winter of 1963, he noticed a beautiful young woman in a drugstore near his home. She was a college student named Vera Cristina Zabala. Roberto asked her out on a date and, even though Vera didn't know at first that Roberto was a baseball hero, she eventually agreed to meet him. Appropriately, the couple spent their first date by going to a baseball game at San Juan's Hiram Bithorn Stadium. Nearly a year later, on November 14, 1964, Roberto and Vera married. The newlyweds moved to Pittsburgh for the 1965 season and began making a home away from home for themselves. In a few years' time, the couple would have three sons: Roberto Jr., Luis, and Enrique, whom they called Ricky.

Roberto and Vera Clemente after their wedding ceremony

MAN OF THE PEOPLE

The young boy who was born poor in the little town of Carolina had grown up to live his dream as a major league baseball player in the United States. Yet he never forgot where he came from. Although he and Vera lived in Pittsburgh during the baseball season, Roberto insisted that when Vera was pregnant she return to the island

Breaking Barriers

By the early 1960s, many outstanding Hispanic players had gained positions on major league rosters and were having an impact. To recognize this trend, the first (and last) Hispanic Major League All-Star Game was played on October 12, 1963. The National League team beat the American League team, 5-2, at the Polo Grounds in New York. The game, which featured five future Hall of Famers, included Roberto Clemente, Orlando Cepeda, and Vic Power, from Puerto Rico; Zoilo Versalles and Tony Oliva, from Cuba; Julian Javier, from the Dominican Republic; and Luis Aparicio, from Venezuela. The NL starter Juan Marichal (Dominican Republic) struck out six batters in four innings, though reliever Al McBean (Virgin Islands) got the win after pinch hitter Manny Mota (Dominican Republic) drove in two runs against losing pitcher Pedro Ramos (Cuba).

Orlando Cepeda was another Hispanic star to find success in the major leagues.

to give birth to their children on Puerto Rican soil. That way another generation of Clementes would be citizens of Puerto Rico.

The Clemente family was excited about the future, and so were Pittsburgh fans. The Pirates had added new, capable players, and Clemente soon would emerge from his shell and become a leader of a small, but growing, group of Hispanic teammates that included infielders Jose Pagan, Jackie Hernandez, and Andre Rodgers, outfielders Matty Alou and Manny Mota, and pitchers Al McBean and Juan Pizarro. All the Latin American play-

Roberto and Vera Clemente instilled a sense of Puerto Rican pride in their sons Luis, Roberto Jr., and Ricky.

ers on the Pirates and their families eventually moved into the Pennley Park apartment complex. A close-knit team was forming.

As Clemente earned the respect of his peers, he was also being praised as an athlete who cared about people. There were always requests for him to visit a hospital, to deliver a speech, or to make a benefit appearance. In his speeches, he would talk of his pride in being a Puerto Rican and of the opportunities in Puerto Rico for those willing to work for them. Because he believed that playing sports builds good character, he gave endlessly of his time and money to help boys in Puerto Rico who wanted to play baseball. He often gave clinics on the island.

"I like to get kids together," he'd say, "and talk to them about the importance of sports, the importance of being a good citizen, the importance of respecting their parents.

"Baseball is a great game," he would tell the young players at the clinics. "The game can do a lot for you, but only when you give it all you can."

Clemente continued to play well in the major leagues, frightening pitchers and keeping base runners from trying to advance. He won the NL batting title again in 1964, when he hit .339, and once more in 1965, batting .329. He was also an uncanny situational hitter. If there were two outs and the Pirates needed a run, he would try to hit a home run. But if his team trailed by three runs, he would just try to hit a single to get on base in the hopes of starting a rally. And when on base, Clemente was able to do what base runners were usually unable to do when he was in the outfield—take the extra base. Clemente was a confident and daring base runner, who knew when to stop and when to run.

"ARRIBA! ARRIBA!"

Clemente could contribute to winning a game in more ways than anyone else in baseball, and he displayed a fierce team spirit that inspired the people of Pittsburgh. The fans now fully embraced Clemente as their favorite player. They admired him because he did everything with style, grace, and flair. Whether running, throwing, or batting, he played as if every moment was a stage show and he was performing just for them.

"*Arriba! Arriba!*" screamed the Pittsburgh fans whenever Roberto had a chance to impact the game. Literally translated into English, "*arriba*" means "upstairs." In the context of a ball game, the fans were encouraging Clemente to lift their team to greater heights. More often than not, he obliged by stealing a base or making a diving catch.

Roberto Clemente proudly signing autographs for his young fans

> **Clemente and His Fans**
>
> Fans called him "The Great One," and the adoration was mutual. On the day of a game, Clemente would go to the ballpark early and remain late, talking to fans and signing autographs.
>
> "I sign 20,000 autographs a year," he once said. "I feel proud when a kid asks for my autograph. I believe we owe something to the people who watch us. They work hard for their money."

31

CHAPTER 6

LEADING BY EXAMPLE

Before the start of the 1966 season, Pirates manager Harry Walker instructed Clemente to swing for the fences more often. He responded with career highs in home runs (29) and runs batted in (119) and sparked the Pirates to a surprisingly high finish, three games out of first place. Success was that much sweeter for Clemente when he won the league's MVP award, the first player from Puerto Rico to be so honored. Clemente was finally earning the respect that he deserved.

In 1967, he won another batting title—his fourth—with a .357 average, and he blasted 23 homers and drove in 110 runs. He was now a mature 13-year veteran in the majors, and he was aware that kids looked up to him as a role model. If an umpire's decision went against him, he found that it was better to keep his composure than to lose his temper. He also showed his dedication to being a team player. When he belted three home runs and knocked in all seven runs in an 8-7 loss to the Reds at Cincinnati's Crosley Field, he would not admit that the performance was satisfying to him. "That was my biggest game," he said, "but not my best game. My best game is when I drive in the winning run. I don't count this one. We lost."

Roberto Clemente batting in 1967, the season he won his fourth league batting title

32

HELPING OTHERS

Clemente helped to pave the way for young Hispanic players, such as the Pirates' catcher Manny Sanguillen, of Panama, by helping them adjust to life in the big leagues. When they came to Pittsburgh, Clemente arranged for them to find places to live, and if they had family, he went out of his way to speak with their wives and children whenever he saw them at the ballpark. Clemente knew they needed help fitting in, just as he had needed help years earlier. He also worked to promote the presence of Latinos in baseball, sharing the spotlight and providing a way for Latino teammates to make more money. Whenever he was asked to appear at a banquet, he agreed to go only if a lesser-known Latino player was also invited to accompany him. Clemente always evenly divided the payment for the appearance with the younger player.

"He was the most decent man I ever met," said Steve Blass, a teammate of Clemente's for nine years, "yet somehow no one seemed to understand him."

Roberto Clemente helped teammates such as Manny Sanguillen (above) of Panama adjust to life in the big leagues.

THE CHANGING TIMES

Racial relations and issues of personal freedom were hot topics during the latter part of the 1960s. The heavyweight champion boxer Cassius Clay became a Muslim, changed his name to Muhammad Ali, and refused to register for the military draft in 1967, and was stripped of his title. The black American sprinters Tommie Smith and John Carlos staged a protest on the medal stand at

Tommie Smith and John Carlos protesting racism on the medal stand at the 1968 Olympics

the 1968 Olympics, raising black-gloved fists to make their point against racism.

There had been outstanding Latino players in the big leagues before Clemente, such as Minnie Minoso and Chico Carrasquel, but they played in the 1950s, when minority players feared losing their jobs if they spoke out against racism. But the times were changing, and Clemente's inner strength gave him the courage to carry the flag for all Latin American countries and to lead Latinos in search of recognition and respect. "For me, he is the Jackie Robinson of Latin baseball," said Ozzie Guillen of Venezuela, a former major league shortstop and now the manager of the Chicago White Sox. "He lived with racism. He was happy not only to be Puerto Rican, but Latin American. He let people know it, and that is very important for all of us."

By the late 1960s, blacks and Hispanics on the Pirates no longer had to travel or eat separately from their white teammates. But racism still existed in baseball. The minority athlete needed more talent than the white athlete to be in the starting lineup, and second-stringers were almost exclusively white athletes. Minority players were paid less money than whites of comparable ability, and certain positions on the field that required intelligence, judgment, authority, and responsibility were almost automati-

Politics or Baseball?

The citizens of San Juan, Puerto Rico once asked him to run for mayor, but Clemente declined, knowing that the baseball field was his best platform from which to effect change.

34

cally considered "white only." In baseball, "thinking" positions, such as catcher, were virtually banned to minorities. And few minority players were represented on the pitcher's mound.

> ### Respecting a Man's Name
>
> Roberto Clemente corrected anyone who Anglicized his name by calling him Bob or Bobby. Even late into the 1960s baseball cards listed him as "Bob Clemente," irritating him greatly. It showed Clemente that while the world of professional sports offered great opportunity to an athlete, it did not necessarily offer respect for his Latino heritage.

MAKING A STAND

To fight against intolerance, Clemente joined with the many people in the **civil rights** movement who were trying to improve the lives of all minorities. Dr. Martin Luther King Jr., a reverend who preached that you can make changes without violence, was the most persuasive speaker for equal rights. Sadly, on April 4, 1968, an assassin shot Dr. King dead. Many baseball teams were scheduled to play their season openers the following day. Although the commissioner of baseball at that time, William Eckert, suggested that teams postpone their opening games in honor of Dr. King, the final decision to play or not was left up to the individual teams. The Pirates were scheduled to open their season in Texas against the Houston Astros. The Pirates management said the decision was up to Houston, as the home team. Roberto Clemente led a group of players on the Pirates who issued a statement saying that they would not play regardless of Houston's decision. "We are doing this because white and black players respect what Dr. King has done for mankind," said Clemente.

A DECADE OF DOMINANCE

No other player dominated the 1960s the way Clemente did. In addition to his four batting titles and the MVP award, he was the major league leader in hits (1,877) and batting average (.328) during the decade. Clemente joined the likes of Hank Aaron, Willie Mays, and Mickey Mantle in the ranks of the top achievers in all of baseball, but he was perhaps the least known superstar in the game. He believed that his Hispanic background was the reason why he was often overlooked by the national media. The Pirates manager during Clemente's early years points out that another factor—geography—may have contributed to the neglect. "If he were playing in New York they'd be comparing him to [Joe] DiMaggio," said Bobby Bragan. "His greatness is limited by the fact that he is not playing in New York, or even Chicago or Los Angeles."

Roberto Clemente continued both to speak out against injustice and to speak up to promote Latin American pride. "He was a person who would defend minorities," said former teammate Manny Mota. "He

Roberto Clemente, Willie Mays, and Hank Aaron at the 1961 All-Star Game. Mays, Clemente, and Aaron were the three best National League players of the decade.

was a leader and controversial because he didn't permit injustices in regards to race. He was very vocal, and that was difficult. He was very misunderstood. But he would not accept injustices with Latins or with players of color. He was always there to defend them." Clemente also continued to play well for the Pirates. Though they were rarely contenders for the title, he remained among the league's best players. As the 1970s began, Clemente was growing older and nearing the end of a glorious career. There would not be many more opportunities for the spotlight, and he desperately wanted another occasion to shine.

NIGHT OF HONOR

The 1970 season was a bittersweet one for Pittsburgh baseball fans. The Pirates' longtime home, Forbes Field, was closed in July and the Pirates started playing in Three Rivers Stadium. On July 24, the team and the city honored their longtime star with "Roberto Clemente Night." Among the gifts he received was a scroll sent from Puerto Rico that had been signed by 300,000 people—nearly 10 percent of the island's population. The event was beamed by satellite back to Puerto Rico. With his wife and children at his side, Clemente addressed the crowd in Spanish and proved to all that he was proud to be both a Puerto Rican and an American. "In a way, I was born twice," he said. "I was born in 1934 and again in 1955, when I came to Pittsburgh. I am thankful I can say that I live two lives."

Pittsburgh fans cheering for the Pirates on a balcony overlooking Forbes Field

Stars like Willie Stargell helped bring the pennant back to Pittsburgh in the early 1970s.

BREAKING NEW GROUND

The Pirates won the 1970 NL Eastern Division title, with Clemente batting .352 for the season—a spectacular average for a 36-year-old. The Pirates lost to the Cincinnati Reds in the new playoff system, but the future looked bright. As the 1971 season began, the Pirates were the team to beat. They had surrounded their veteran star with terrific young players, including sluggers Willie Stargell, Bob Robertson, and Al Oliver and pitching aces Dock Ellis and Steve Blass. In addition to winning games, the Pirates were breaking new ground as an equal opportunity employer. They often fielded a starting lineup with more minority players— including both blacks and Latinos— than whites. Clemente was proud to be their leader. "We must all live together and work together, no matter what race or nationality," he said.

Historic Scorecard

On September 1, 1971, the Pirates fielded the first all-black lineup in the one-hundred-year history of major league baseball, in a 10–7 win over the Phillies. The lineup:

Rennie Stennett, 2B
Gene Clines, CF
Roberto Clemente, RF
Willie Stargell, LF
Manny Sanguillen, C
Dave Cash, 3B
Al Oliver, 1B
Jackie Hernandez, SS
Dock Ellis, P

HITTING THE BIG TIME

CHAPTER 7

Playing like a team that was ready to step up to the next level, the Pirates earned another trip to the playoffs after the 1971 season. With Clemente hitting .333 and driving in four runs, they knocked off the San Francisco Giants in the NL Championship Series and made it to the World Series for the first time since 1960.

Roberto Clemente's clutch home run in the 1971 World Series propelled the Pirates to the championship.

THE GREAT ONE

Clemente approached the World Series match-up against the Baltimore Orioles with a strong sense of purpose. At thirty-seven years old, this would likely be his final appearance on baseball's biggest stage. It was his chance to prove, once and for all, that he was a clutch player and a team leader.

Pittsburgh and Baltimore split the first six games of the series. In the dramatic Game Seven, Clemente hit a home run to give the Pirates a lead and propel them to victory. The Pirates were world champions, and Clemente was the star. During the Series, he batted .414 with two homers and four RBIs. In the field, he made fifteen **putouts** and an amazing throw to keep a runner from scoring that remains one of the best defensive plays in World Series history. Clemente was named the MVP of the World Series, hands down.

This time, Clemente celebrated with his teammates, and as he stood on the podium to accept his trophy, he told a worldwide television audience what the other players already knew. "I want everyone in the world to know that this is the way I play all of the time," he said. "All season. Every season."

Then Clemente had an important message to deliver to his parents, who were watching from San Juan. He said, "I want to say something in Spanish to my mother and father. *En este, el momento más grande de mi vida, les pido la benedición.* At this, the greatest moment of my life, I ask your blessing."

After the season, Clemente returned to Puerto Rico to manage a team of Puerto Rican baseball stars that traveled around Latin America playing exhibition games. He also announced plans to build a sports complex for the youngsters of Puerto Rico. "I like to work with kids," he told Sports Illustrated in 1966. "I'd like to work with kids all the time, if I live long enough."

Roberto Clemente celebrating in the locker room after the Pirates won the 1971 World Series

ANOTHER RECORD

Although age and injuries began to catch up with Clemente, he returned for the 1972 season to compete for another pennant and to chase an important milestone: 3,000 career hits. At the time, only ten players in baseball history had reached that mark. Facing New York Mets pitcher

Ten Hits In Two Days

There were so many sparkling performances in Clemente's career that it is impossible to select the single most amazing game. But you could pick the most amazing *two* games! On August 22 and August 23, 1970, Clemente became the first player to get five hits in a game—in two games in a row. He went five for seven in a sixteen-inning night game and came back with five more hits the next day. Normally, Clemente, who was thirty-six at the time, would have been rested after a long game, but because some of his teammates were injured, he asked Danny Murtaugh to keep him in the lineup.

"Roberto really should not have played that second game," recalled Murtaugh. "He was so tired from the previous night's game and lack of sleep, that he passed up batting practice. But he played all twenty-five innings within a twenty-hour period. . . . Man, when I was playing, it would take me three or four weeks to get that many hits."

John Matlack on September 30, Clemente hit a line drive to the left-field wall for a double—his 3,000th hit. He was the first player from Latin America to reach that mark. Nobody knew it at the time, but it would be his last regular-season hit. He had four more hits in the Pirates' loss to the Cincinnati Reds in the playoffs and then he headed to Puerto Rico for the winter.

TRAGIC END

On December 23, an earthquake rocked Managua, the capital city of Nicaragua. Much of the city was leveled, thousands of people were killed or injured, and even more were left homeless. Devastated, Clemente organized a relief campaign and called for Puerto Ricans to come to the aid of their fellow Hispanics. Tons of food,

Umpire Doug Harvey handing the ball to Roberto Clemente after his 3,000th hit

Managua, Nicaragua, was in ruins after an earthquake struck the city two days before Christmas in 1972.

clothing, and medical supplies were donated and sent to Nicaragua, but the supplies were being stolen before reaching the people in need. Determined to make sure the people got the help they needed, Clemente decided to go Nicaragua and deliver the goods himself.

On December 31, 1972, just three months after his historic 3,000th hit, Clemente went to San Juan's Luis Munoz Marin Airport and boarded a cargo plane taking supplies to Nicaragua. The plane never made it there, crashing into the Atlantic Ocean shortly after takeoff. There were no survivors. Family and friends were shocked but took comfort in the fact that Clemente had died on a mission to help others. All of Puerto Rico, and all of baseball, was saddened to lose one of its noblest heroes at such a young age.

New Year's Day was to have been a day of celebration, but as people heard the tragic news of Clemente's death, many gathered on the beach at Isla Verde to light a candle for their national hero. The entire Pirates team traveled to Puerto Rico for the funeral.

Three months after the death of Roberto Clemente, America's baseball writers held a special meeting. A player must be out of baseball for at least five years before he can be voted into the Hall of Fame. The writers decided to break the rule and vote Clemente into the Hall of Fame immediately. He was the first Latino player to become a member of this elite group. Clemente was inducted into the Hall of Fame at a ceremony on August 8, 1973—the same day as one of his boyhood idols, Monte Irvin.

THE CLEMENTE LEGACY

In 1971, major league baseball owners started giving an annual award to the player who best demonstrates outstanding service to the community; in 1973, this award was renamed the Roberto Clemente Award. One recent winner was Sammy Sosa of the Chicago Cubs. There are also hospitals in Puerto Rico named for Clemente, as well as schools in Latin America and the United States that bear his name.

One of Clemente's greatest dreams was realized after his tragic death. Enough money was donated in his memory to enable the Clemente family to build the *Ciudad Deportiva*, or Sports City, near San Juan. Today, thousands of Puerto Rican children enjoy sports facilities that Clemente never had as a kid. So, even though Roberto Clemente is gone, he is still helping others.

Today's major league rosters are filled with talented players from the Caribbean and South American countries. Superstars such as Sammy Sosa, Pedro Martinez, Albert Pujols, Bernie Williams, and others might indeed have become heroes on their own, but one thing is for certain: the path they traveled was paved by what Roberto Clemente did for baseball and for the Latin American people.

Getting the Name Right

At first, the Hall of Fame plaque listed his name as Roberto Walker Clemente. But this was changed in 2000. In the Hispanic and Latino cultures, a person's mother's maiden name traditionally follows the given last name. So the Hall of Fame corrected the cultural oversight and changed the plaque to read Roberto Clemente Walker.

Roberto Clemente's original Hall of Fame plaque. A corrected plaque was issued in 2000.

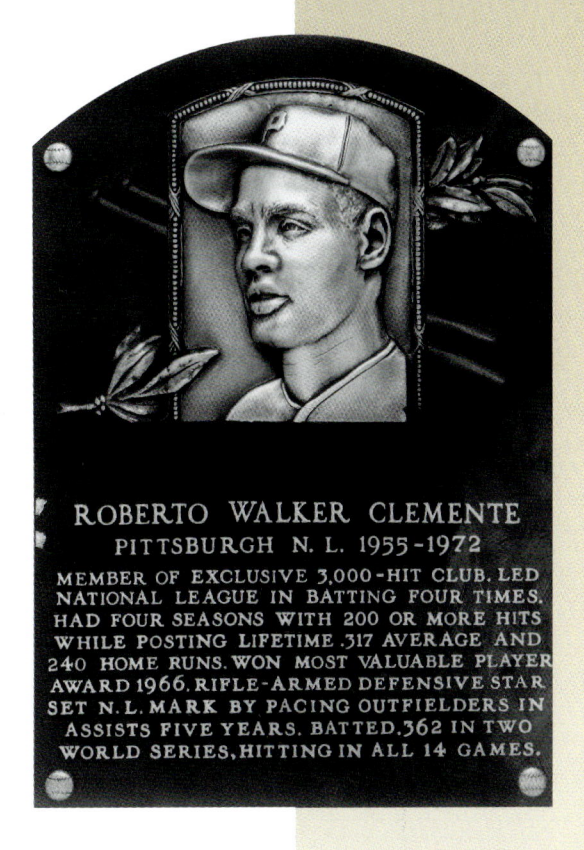

ROBERTO WALKER CLEMENTE
PITTSBURGH N.L. 1955-1972
MEMBER OF EXCLUSIVE 3,000-HIT CLUB. LED NATIONAL LEAGUE IN BATTING FOUR TIMES. HAD FOUR SEASONS WITH 200 OR MORE HITS WHILE POSTING LIFETIME .317 AVERAGE AND 240 HOME RUNS. WON MOST VALUABLE PLAYER AWARD 1966. RIFLE-ARMED DEFENSIVE STAR SET N.L. MARK BY PACING OUTFIELDERS IN ASSISTS FIVE YEARS. BATTED .362 IN TWO WORLD SERIES, HITTING IN ALL 14 GAMES.

TIMELINE

1934	Roberto Clemente Walker is born on August 18 in Carolina, Puerto Rico
1948	Discovered by scout Roberto Marín
1952	Signs first professional contract with the Santurce Cangrejeros (Crabbers) of the Puerto Rican League.
1954	Signs a contract with the Brooklyn Dodgers and comes to the United States; plays for the Montreal Royals and in November is drafted by the Pittsburgh Pirates
1955	Plays first game for the Pittsburgh Pirates on April 17; singles in his first major league at bat
1960	Pirates defeat the New York Yankees to win the World Series; Clemente hits safely in all seven game
1961	Wins first of twelve Gold Glove awards; plays in first All-Star Game; wins first batting title
1964	Marries Vera Cristina Zabala; wins second National League batting title
1965	Wins third batting title
1966	Named Most Valuable Player for the National League
1967	Wins fourth and final batting title
1970	Honored with Roberto Clemente Night at Three Rivers Stadium in Pittsburgh
1971	Pirates defeat the Baltimore Orioles to win the World Series; named the Most Valuable Player of the series
1972	Collects his 3,000th and final career hit; dies on December 31 in a plane crash while leaving Puerto Rico
1973	Inducted into the Baseball Hall of Fame; Pirates retire "21" jersey; award for baseball humanitarian renamed in his honor
1994	Statue of Clemente unveiled outside Three Rivers Stadium
1999	The Sixth Street Bridge in Pittsburgh is renamed the Roberto Clemente Bridge
2002	On September 18, Major League Baseball celebrates Roberto Clemente Day

GLOSSARY

assists: plays in baseball in which a fielder throws the ball to a base to get a runner out; also the statistic credited to fielders who make this type of play

barrio: a part of a city or town populated by Spanish-speaking people

bigotry: a strong dislike of certain groups of people, usually racially motivated

civil rights: equal rights and freedoms for all citizens

discrimination: unjust treatment of people based on race, background, or religion

farm team: a minor league team, usually affiliated with a major league team for the purpose of developing younger players

hypochondriac: a person with imaginary pains or illnesses

javelin: a light metal spear used in athletic contests for distance throwing

major league baseball: North American professional baseball played in the National League and the American League

pennant: the championship title of a baseball league; in the major leagues, the winners of the individual pennants face each other in the World Series

phenomenon: something or someone extraordinarily unique

putouts: plays in baseball in which a fielder catches a ball hit by a batter to get the batter out; also the statistics credited to fielders who make this type of play.

racists: people who believe that one race is superior to all others and judge others on the basis of their race

rookie: a first-year professional athlete

scout: a person sent to observe athletes and report on their abilities

TO FIND OUT MORE

BOOKS

Dunham, Montrew. **Roberto Clemente: Young Baseball Player (Childhood of Famous Americans)**. New York: Simon and Schuster, 1997.

Engel, Trudie. **We'll Never Forget You, Roberto Clemente**. New York: Scholastic, 1997.

Gilbert, Thomas W. **Roberto Clemente (Hispanics of Achievement)**. Broomall, Penn.: Chelsea House, 1995.

Macht, Norman L. **Roberto Clemente: Baseball Hero (Junior World Biographies)**. Broomall, Penn.: Chelsea House, 1994.

Markusen, Bruce. **Roberto Clemente: The Great One**. Champaign, Ill.: Sports Publishing, 1998.

Walker, Paul Robert. **Pride of Puerto Rico: The Life of Roberto Clemente**. San Diego, Calif.: Harcourt, Brace, Jovanovich, 1989.

INTERNET SITES

The Official Roberto Clemente Website
http://www.robertoclemente21.com
A site sponsored by the Roberto Clemente Foundation that chronicles Clemente's life and accomplishments. Includes family photos and a 3,000th hit tribute.

The Roberto Clemente Foundation
http://www.robertoclementefoundation.org/pages/798673/index.htm
Information about the charity founded in Roberto Clemente's name; also includes biographical information.

The National Baseball Hall of Fame
http://www.baseballhalloffame.org/index.htm
Information about the Hall of Fame and all of its honorees.

Latino Baseball
http://www.latinobaseball.com
Mostly in Spanish, but includes historical articles in English about Latino baseball stars of the past and present.

INDEX

Page numbers in *italics* indicate illustrations.

Aaron, Hank 36, *36*
Ali, Muhammad 33
Alou, Matty 29
Angell, Roger 4
Aparicio, Luis 29

Baltimore Orioles 39
Baptists 9
Baseball Hall of Fame 42, 43, *43*
Bierbauer, Lou 20
Blass, Steve 33, 38
Bragan, Bobby 36
Brooklyn Dodgers 10, 14–16

Campanis, Al 14–15
Canada 15
Carlos, John 33–34, *34*
Carrasquel, Chico 34
Cepeda, Orlando 29, *29*
Chicago Cubs 43
Chicago White Sox 34
Cincinnati Reds 32, 38, 41
civil rights movement 33–35
Clarkson, James Buster "Buzz" 13
Clemente, Enrique (son) 28, *30*
Clemente, Luis (son) 28, *30*
Clemente, Luisa (mother) 7–9, *8*, 11, *25*, 40
Clemente, Melchor (father) 7–9, *8*, 11, 40
Clemente, Roberto
   as base runner 30–31
   batting titles won by 26, 30, 32, *32*
   commemorative stamp *5*
   dealings with umpires 23, *23*, 32
   dies in plane crash 41–42
   dislike of being called Bob or Bobby 35
   as dominant figure in 1960s baseball 36, *36*
   fielding prowess *21*, 21–22
   Hall of Fame induction 42, 43, *43*
   has ten hits in 2 days 41
   injuries sustained by *26*, 26–27
   as javelin thrower 12
   King assassination reaction 35–36
   legacy of 43
   marriage of 28, *28*
   as minor leaguer 15–16
   as National League MVP 32
   as Pittsburgh fan favorite 31, *31*
   as Puerto Rican hero 20, 42
   Puerto Rican pride felt by 28–29, *30*
   racial discrimination faced by 16–18, 23
   reaches 3,000 hits 4, *4*, 40–41, *41*
   refusal to enter Puerto Rican politics 34
   as role model for Latin players 33, 34, 36–37, 43
   rookie season *19*, 20–21
   strained media relations 25, 26, 36
   trouble learning English 18–19, 23
   as World Series MVP (1971) *39*, 39–40, *40*
Clemente Jr., Roberto (son) 28, *30*
Clemente, Vera (wife) 22, 28, *28*, *30*
Columbus, Christopher 6
Crosley Field (Cincinnati) 32

Delorimier Downs (Montreal) 16
DiMaggio, Joe 36

Ebbets Field (Brooklyn, N.Y.) 15
Eckert, William 35
Ellis, Dock 38

Fenway Park (Boston) 10
Forbes Field (Pittsburgh) 37, *37*

Gold Glove Awards 4, 22, *22*
Groat, Dick 25
Guillen, Ozzie 34

Harvey, Doug *41*
Hernandez, Jackie 29
Hispanic Major League All-Star Game (1963) 29
Houston Astros 35

Irvin, Monte 11, *11*, 42

Jackson, Al 18
javelin throwing 12
Javier, Julian 29

King Jr., Dr. Martin Luther 35–36
King, Nellie 19, *27*

Los Angeles Dodgers 41
Luis Munoz Marin Airport (San Juan) 42

Macon, Max 16
Managua earthquake (1972) 41–42, *42*
Marichal, Juan 29
Marin, Roberto 12
Martinez, Pedro 43
Matlack, John 4, 41
Mays, Willie 14, *14*, 22, 36, *36*
Mazeroski, Bill 23–24, *24*
McBean, Al 29
Mickey, Mantle 36
Milwaukee Braves 15
Minoso, Minnie 34
Montreal Royals 15–16
Mota, Manny 29, 36
Murtaugh, Danny 27, *27*, 41

Negro Leagues 10, 11, 13, 14
New York Mets 4, 40
New York Yankees 23
Nicaragua *see* Managua earthquake (1972)

Oliva, Tony 29
Oliver, Al 38
Olympic Games 12, 34, *34*

Pagan, Jose 29
Philadelphia Athletics 20

47

INDEX (continued)

Pittsburgh Pirates
  Clemente drafted by *18*, 19
  first all-black lineup fielded 38
  Latin American contingent 29–30
  as NL Eastern Division winners (1970) 38
  as NL Eastern Division winners (1972) 41
  origin of name 20
  as small market team 36
  as World Series champs (1960) 23–25
  as World Series champs (1971) *39*, 39–40
Pizarro, Juan 29
Polo Grounds (New York City) 29
Power, Vic 29
Puerto Rican Winter League 10, 11, 13, 28
Puerto Rico
  baseball in 10
  as Clemente birthplace 5, 7
  Clemente scroll signed by 10% of population 37

  as Clemente sons' birthplace 28–29
  facts on 6
  Sports City completion 43
Pujols, Albert 43

racism
  in baseball 10
  in society at large 16–17, *17*
  struggle against 33–35
Ramos, Pedro 29
Rickey, Branch *18*, 19
Roberto Clemente Award 43
"Roberto Clemente Night" 37
Roberts, Curt 20
Robertson, Bob 38
Robinson, Jackie 10, *10*, 34
Rodgers, Andre 29
Roman Catholicism 9

Sanguillen, Manny 33, *33*
Santurce Cangrejeros (Crabbers) *13*, 13–14, *14*
Scully, Vin 21
Sello Rojo Rice Company 12

Sixto Escobar Stadium (San Juan) 11
Smith, Tommie 33–34, *34*
Sosa, Sammy 43
Spain 6
Spanish-American War (1898) 10
Sports City (Puerto Rico) 43
Sports Illustrated (magazine) 40
Stargell, Willie 22, 38, *38*
sugar cane 7, *7*, 8
Sukeforth, Clyde 19

Three Rivers Stadium (Pittsburgh) 4, 37
Thurman, Bob 14

Versalles, Zoilo 29
Vizcarrondo High School 12

Walker, Harry 32
Williams, Bernie 43
World Series 4, 23–25, *24*, *39*, 39–40

Yankee Stadium (New York City) 10

About the Author

David Fischer is the author of *The Story of the New York Yankees*, *The Encyclopedia of the Summer Olympics,* and *Do Curve Balls Really Curve?* His freelance articles have appeared in *The New York Times* and *Sports Illustrated for Kids*, and he has worked for *Sports Illustrated*, *NBC Sports*, and *The National* sports daily.